You always hold my hand

Prayers for everyday life.

Jules Beaulac

LEVAIN
205 West, Laurier Street
MONTREAL, Qc. H2T 2N9

Legal deposit - 1986 - National Library of Canada
- National Library of Quebec

First printing: August 1986
Second printing May 1987

ISBN 2-920556-09-6

When you want to pray, all you have to do is to get in touch with God dwelling in you. Knock at the door of your heart. He is right there. You will find him in the bottomless depths of your heart. "Do you not know your body is a shrine of the indwelling Holy Spirit?" (I Corinthians 6, 19). Do you realize Jesus and his Father yearn to come to you and dwell within you (John 14, 23)?

When you want to pray, go into a quiet and peaceful room by yourself (Matthew 6, 6). Stand in the presence of Almighty God and talk with him. Tell him everything about your own life, joys, hardships, hopes, sufferings and the like. Speak to him about those whom you love, those who love you and the others whom you love less or not at all. Disclose your own sincere love for him. Then, keep silence. Listen to him telling you: "I have always loved you and I will never forget you."

When you pray, let your soul breathe in and out. Thus, you will bring your heart into harmony with the heart of God and the hearts of the Church and the world at the same time. Refill your heart with energy, strength, so you can keep going forward on the sometimes difficult road of life.

You can pray as often as you wish and wherever you wish. Sometimes, you go to church to unite yourself to the prayer of your brothers and sisters in the faith. But you can also pray in your car, in the elevator, in your kitchen, walking on the street. The Lord, who is in your heart, is your most faithful companion. You have only to make contact with him.

Let your prayer rise just as you feel, like fragrant incense (Psalm 141, 2). At one time you may say, "Thank you, you are my best friend, I belong to you, you make me happy." Sometimes you will entreat him to help you move forward through your sufferings and solitude. Then other times you will whisper, "I have sinned against you, forgive me, heal my wounds."

If you pray this way, in the great moments of your life as well as in the everyday happenings, you will feel inner peace pervading and abiding in you. Your heart will expand with love, and joy will give your life heavenly flavors.

At dawn, I celebrate your love.
Psalm 59. 17

8

Morning prayer

Lord,
the sun is rising.
The sunshine is already coming
through the window into my room.
It will be a wonderful day.

I offer you this day
as it begins.
Bless those people
I shall meet today.
May I be their sunshine,
a sign of your presence.

And may your peace,
your deep and wonderful peace,
fill us to our very depths.
Amen.

My dear people,
we are already the children of God.

1 John 3, 2

Suffering

Almighty Father,
I know somewhere in the world
a man is suffering intensely.

His best friend has betrayed him,
his brothers have abandoned him,
his close relations have hurt him.

He suffers in silence, alone.
In prayer he suffers too,
since he is a man of prayer.

There is no confidant available;
everybody seems heedless of his worries,
but, only you, Lord.

Come to his aid.
Give him comfort and peace.
Send a Good Samaritan on his path.

Watch over him.
He is your child.

Amen.

You shall love.
Luke 10, 27

Love

Dear God!
May love in me be powerful, strong, beautiful,
yet also gentle, tender and simple.

May I be able to smile at those who are unhappy,
offer a helping hand to those who are hurt,
and hold those who are sad in my arms.

May I also be able to close my eyes to insults
and my ears to slander,
but never my heart to anyone.

Lastly, if I know how to give,
may I also know how to accept
from those who want to love me in return.

For the lover who knows how to love
can never be radiant
if he does not know how to be loved.

Amen.

The Lord has forgiven you, do the same.
Colossians 3, 13

How to forgive?

Lord Jesus,
a friend of mine has hurt me so badly
that I really think
I will never be able to forgive him.

When I think of the harm he has done to me:
my reputation seriously tarnished,
my health endangered,
my friendship brutally broken,
I get angry and I cry about it.
My heart is full of resentment,
I'm full of bitterness.
I'm rigid with vengeance.
How can I forgive him?
It's too much, too hard!
How can you ask me to forgive him?
Help me!
I cannot forget all he has done to me.
It haunts my memory too much
and above all my heart is hurt, wounded, broken.

Give me your peace,
calm the storm.
Give me something of your heart.
I cannot do it without you.

Do not be afraid!

Revelation 1, 17

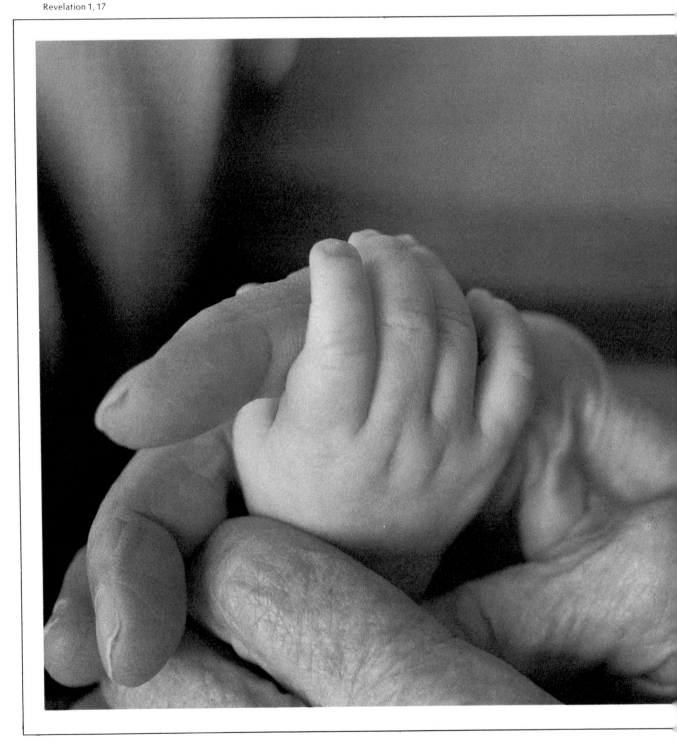

I need you badly

Father,
keep me near you.
Do not leave me.
I need you badly,
on days of sunshine and light,
and especially
on nights
of darkness and suffering.

I rely on you.
Hold my hand.
Comfort me.
Guide me.
I can do nothing without you.

Amen.

Each time you have helped one of the least of my brothers,
it is me you have helped.

Matthew 25, 40

Jesus' brothers and sisters

O Lord Jesus,
how deeply you love all those
who lead toilful lives:
the hungry, the thirsty, the lonely,
the sick, the prisoners, the poor...
It is so true that you identify yourself with them,
and you want us to recognize you in them!

They are so full of dignity to your eyes,
all these wretched and suffering people:
the unloved, unwelcome ones
whom no one visits, no one listens to...
They mean so much to you
that it is about this and only about this
that you will question us
when we come before you
at the end of our lives.

You do not want us to forget them,
all these castaways:
the despised, the dejected, the forgotten,
those who are ugly, dirty, uninteresting...
You are more concerned
about the good we have not done to them
than about the evil we have done!

O Lord,
give us a little of your heart
so we may love them as you love them!

God, be merciful to the sinner that I am.

Luke 18, 13

This craving for you

Lord,

You walked along the road to Emmaus
with two disciples who were despondent and desperate.
In my hours of doubt and distress, walk with me too.
Show me your word, feed me with your bread.

You accepted the invitation to eat with Simon the Pharisee,
with Levi the crook, with Zaccheus the thief.
Come to visit me too,
share my meal, come to my home.
I am no better than they were.

You forgave Peter the turncoat, Judas the traitor,
Magdalene the public sinner.
Forgive the sinner I am,
I who have so often paid no attention to you
on the paths of evil.

You healed the blind man, the deaf, the lame,
you cleansed the leper,
you freed the man possessed by an evil spirit.
Let me realize it is useless to try
to understand everything,
to explain everything, direct everything.
May I rely on you in everything,
may I accept myself as a gift from you.
And above all may I always crave for you.

Amen.

Look at the lilies of the field.
Matthew 6, 28

Getting used to things

Holy Spirit,
we become so used to your wonders
that we end up seeing them no longer.
We stop admiring, we stop being amazed.
And yet... we should never become used to such beauty.

I have a friend who spent three months in a hospital
in a featureless desert of white.
Everything was white: the walls, the curtains, the nurse, the doctor.
The day he left the hospital,
everything seemed so beautiful to him.
It was as if he had rediscovered everything:
the strength of tall trees, the simplicity of daisies,
the song of a stream, the glory of a sunset,
the smile of his children, the gentleness of his wife.

Perhaps now and again we need a short time of seclusion
so we can better appreciate life, nature, people!

Keep us from getting used to things.
May everything and everyone seem new and beautiful
with you in their midst.

Amen.

Father, let this cup pass away from me.
Matthew 26, 38

Change my heart

O Jesus,
how much you had to suffer in the garden of Gethsemani!
You were hurt enough to utter words of despair,
you sweated drops of blood,
you prayed to exhaustion
and you held out against the cup... as long as you could.

And then little by little you accepted it,
as you could not change it.
It was your heart which you changed
in the midst of the inner battle.
It was not easy.
Your Father helped you greatly.

You see what has happened to me.
For weeks now I have been asking:
"Why should this happen?
Why should it happen to me?"
I too hold out, I too resist.
I pray about it, I complain.
I am angry, I sweat about it.
Must I die of this?
Don't leave me. Come, help me.

Help me.
Change my heart
if what is happening cannot be changed.
And thank you once again.

Do not withhold your kindness from me.

Psalm 40, 11

To be myself

Father,
have pity on me.

Where I live,
it is impossible to show my true self.
I am impelled to wear a mask.
I have had to make a thick shell
and hide my feelings
deep, deep within me.

It is hard to be compelled to live
always hiding my best side.
Because we assume other personalities,
we end up like them.
Because we hide our feelings,
we end up thinking we have none.

You who know the bottom of my heart,
you know what it holds
as to kindness, caring, generosity, courage.
Do not reject me.
Let me be myself
right next to you.

Amen.

For I was hungry and you gave me food.
Matthew 25, 35

Ethiopia

Lord Jesus,
thousands and thousands of children
are dying in Ethiopia.
They have nothing to eat, nothing to drink.
Help comes often too late.
A powerless government.

I want to go to Ethiopia.
I cannot do much.
I have only my arms and my heart
but I want to go to this land of wretchedness.

Perhaps just to take one small, dying child into my arms,
to hold him against my heart,
to give him just a piece of love
so he does not die on the ground like a dog.
And to be well assured
it is you
I hold close to me.

Amen.

See, I have branded your name on the palms of my hands.

Isaiah 49, 16

Tell me once again that you love me

Lord,
tonight I need you
to tell me again that your love of me is still
strong and tender.

Today so many people frustrated me,
I am tired to death.
So many years have slipped away in my life,
I am worn to a thread.
So many wounds have torn my body,
my very bones feel broken.

You said, "Come to me,
all you who labor and are burdened,
and I will give you rest."
Here I am, Lord,
with the weight of my wretchedness,
the burden of my suffering,
the yoke of my sins.
Tell me once more that you love me,
that you will never forsake me.

Amen.

He who does not love abides in death.
1 John 3, 14

Lord, make us...

My God, how many lies are in the world!
Lies of the great and the lowly,
lies of the unsincere and the arrogant,
lies both in and out of the courts...
Lord, make us builders of truth.

My God, how much injustice is in the world!
Injustice caused by the powerful and the weak,
injustice caused by the ambitious and criminals,
injustice at home and in the factory...
Lord, make us workers for justice.

My God, how many wars there are in the world!
Wars between countries and peoples,
wars between churches and religions,
wars between families and individuals...
Lord, make us workers for peace.

My God, how much selfishness there is in the world!
Selfishness among the rich and the powerful,
selfishness among adults and children,
selfishness among institutions and groups...
Lord, let us work toward sharing.

My God, how much hate there is in the world!
Hate between nations and towns,
hate between men and women,
hate between loved and ill-loved...
Lord, make us builders of love.

Amen.

Take off your robe of mourning and misery
and put on the beautiful attire of the glory of God forever.
Baruch 5, 1

Solitude

O God,
I have been in bed
for months now.

At the beginning,
I had visitors.
But, little by little,
all of them have gone away.
They are very busy
and I am no longer interesting:
I have a crooked mouth,
I cannot smile any more,
I can hardly open my mouth and speak.

I do not know
if they will come to see me at Christmas...

Stay near me.
Maintain hope in my heart.
May your peace be with me always.
And give me the strength to understand
and to forgive!

I have come so they may have life and have it to the full.
John 10, 10

Consumer's prayer

Holy Spirit,
publicity, awful publicity,
is always clamoring at us.
It is always with us
in the "new" and the "super".
And we get caught,
too often.
We have become "super-consumers".
We swallow commercial announcements,
almost unwillingly,
since they are so intrusive and fascinating.

Free us from the need for "owning" and "owning more and more".
and let us wish "to be", "to be always more".

Amen.

I am the handmaid of the Lord.
Luke 1, 38

So weak...

O Jesus Christ,
I feel so weak, so powerless,
on this path to which you beckon me.
I feel unworthy of your call and your trust...

Keep me humble.
Increase within me
my confidence in your bounty and tenderness.
Send me your Spirit,
that it may give me light and strength
so I may know exactly and then achieve
what you expect from me.

Amen.

Is it not true that shepherds have to pasture their flocks?
Ezechiel 34, 2

For pastors

Lord Jesus,
I am praying to you
for the shepherds of our churches.

Give them wisdom and strength
that they may guide their sheep
to good pastures,
that they may have the strength
to stand upright in adversity.

Give them enlightenment and watchfulness
that they may be faithful to your word
despite the contradictions of this world,
that they may be able to separate the wheat from the weeds.

Give them enthusiasm and hope
that they may kindle joy
in the hearts of the faithful
and give their sense of life
to all who meet them.

And may their sheep love them
and support them
in their hard yet wonderful work.

Amen.

Turn to me and have pity on me.
Psalm 86, 16

Anxiety

O Father,
I must tell you that for some time
there is something wrong in my mind.

I'm sleeping badly and I know why:
I have in my right side a pain
which doesn't go away,
especially at night.
At first I thought: "It will disappear."
But as time goes on,
I notice it is not going away.
I am worried.
I must see the doctor.
But you know,
we are never in a rush to see a doctor,
especially when we fear bad news.
So I am waiting hopefully.

I have told you my problem.
Help me find out what I ought to do
and give me the courage to do so.

Amen.

Have they not understood, all these evil men?
Psalm 52, 5

Forgive us, Lord

For those fathers and mothers
who beat their children
that they may be quiet
and keep cool... Forgive us!

For those military men
who mindlessly kill both civilians and soldiers,
who rape women and girls,
who slaughter children,
because of war... Forgive us!

For those policemen
who lash out with kicks and blows
on the supposed culprits,
to make them talk,
and on criminals
to teach them not to relapse in crime... Forgive us!

For those delinquents
who break into homes
and attack innocent people on the street
and who make them fearful
for the remainder of their lives... Forgive us!

For those heads of state
who build peace on the strength of their weapons
and who promote a military build-up
because "it must be done"... Forgive us!

For the leaders in those networks of young people
who treat bodies as things
just to make money... Forgive us!

Forgive, Lord, all those who have no respect
for the human person, whoever he or she may be.
Forgive us, Lord, forgive us!

God is love.
1 John 4, 8

I am in love

Beloved Father,
I am in love
and how wonderful it is!
Since I have known him,
nothing seems to be the same.
Everything I do,
everything I live,
is tinted with his presence.
I'm not the same:
it's as if I had wings.
I smile so easily
and I am full of enthusiasm.

You created love.
You are love, nothing but love.
Thank you for the love you give us
and for the love you let us live.
If our love is but a reflection of yours,
how beautiful your love must be.

Amen.

The root of all evil is covetousness.
1 Timothy 6, 10

For just a few more dollars

Lord,
they do not want their aged father
to end his days in a nursing home.
It's not because they want to look after him
nor because they want to cherish him,
but because it would be expensive...
it would take that much money from their inheritance.

It doesn't matter whether their father is well or not.
What matters is that it costs as little as possible.
Such things are revolting and shocking.
Can love be so badly misplaced?
Can human hearts so dry up

Lord,
help those people.
May their hearts not close up for ever and ever
but rather open to charity!
And may I not judge them, despite everything!

Amen.

Stand erect, your liberation is at hand.
Luke 21, 28

Why?

Why, Lord,
are so many people born with so few resources?
Why does Mario need growth hormones to grow taller?
Why does Lucy feel she is more masculine than feminine?
Why has Eric never been loved
and why does he always feel rejected?
Why was Judith born deaf and dumb?
Why was Peter sexually defiled
when he was only six years old?
Why? why? why?

We say you are good as well as powerful.
Why do you let it happen?
Why don't you interfere?

Help me understand,
I can hardly see.
Help me love you,
I am sick at heart.

Amen.

Lord, you know much I love you.
John 21, 15

I love you

I love you, Lord Jesus.
Can I repeat it enough?
I love you.

How could I help loving you
When I see so many wonders of yours in this world?
From the simple flower that grows on the edge of a woods
to the rose in my garden which delights our eyes...
from the white butterfly which flutters from flower to flower
to the powerful eagle which dominates the heights...
from the laugh of a child who enlightens our lives
to the glance of an old man who pacifies our hearts...

Everything around us speaks of you:
the love of young people,
the love between spouses,
also the love of brothers and sisters, and friends...

I see you in nature
and in human beings.
I see your kindness,
your generosity towards us.

And I love you more and more.

Amen.

You formed me from the womb.

Isaiah 49, 5

I am yours

I am yours, Lord.
I am clay in your hands, mould me.
I am your canvas, paint me.

I am yours, Lord.
I am the wood, you are the fire.
I am the rock, you are the wave.
I am the sand, you are the wind.

I am yours, Lord.
I am the tree, you are the sap.
I am the night, you are the star.
I am the stream, your are the spring.

I am yours, Lord.
As the child belongs to his father,
as the fiancé belongs to his beloved,
as the wife to her husband.

And I am happy...

Amen.

Happy are you poor, for the kingdom of God is yours.
Luke 6, 20

Happy is he who cares for the poor and the weak.
Psalm 41, 2

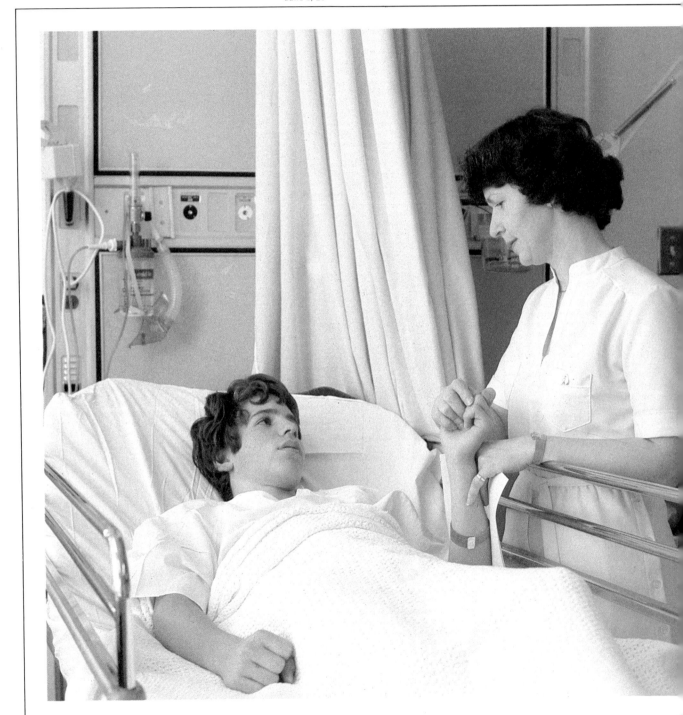

Happy...

Happy are the poor in this world
who are listened to and helped,
welcomed and loved.
Happy are the poor in this world!
And happy are the rich in this world
who share and give,
sow and forgive.
Happy are the rich in this world!

Happy are the lowly on earth
who are respected and recognized,
considered and promoted.
Happy are the lowly on earth!
And happy are the great on earth
who promote and give honors,
acclaim and decorate.
Happy are the great on earth!

Happy are the sick on earth
who are visited and loved,
cared for, looked after.
Happy are the sick on earth!
And happy are the healthy on earth
who comfort and smile,
strengthen and console.
Happy are the healthy on earth!

Happy the one
who sings to the sad,
soothes the weak,
visits the lonely.
Happy the one
who weeps with the unhappy,
suffers with the depressed,
cries out with the oppressed.

Happy the one
who looks for the clear water of truth
and finds it the spirit,
at the winding road.
Happy the one
who looks for friendship
and finds it within his heart,
at the inn on the corner.

Happy the one
who has nothing
and gives it cheerfully.
Happy the one
who possesses much
and shares it without misgivings.
Happy the one
who loves
without asking anything in return.
Happy the one
who helps
without claiming anything.

Happy...!

Jesus looked upon him and loved him.
Mark 10, 21

The young

Father,
how wonderful are all these young people
who have all their lives before them
and ask nothing more than to make others happy!

They encourage me in my work
and comfort me every day.
I admire their confidence in life
as well as their energy and enthusiasm.
How I love to see them busy,
building their lives,
trying to grasp each day
a little more of the great realities of life:
love, death, truth, suffering, sharing.

How good it is to work with them
in building a more human world!

For all of these
you give me to love each day,
thank you, Father.

Amen.

Oh, that you would rend the heavens!

Isaiah 63, 19

Ah! if...

Ah, God,
that you would tear apart my night,
break my chains,
let me jump over the wall...

You know I see no more light
at the end of the tunnel.
I am still dragging this overwhelming weight chained to my ankle.
I wear a leaden coat riveted to my shoulders.

Sometimes I feel I am going
farther down into the depths of hell.
It is as if an iron grip were drawn tighter around my heart,
as if a boa constrictor had wound itself around my body
and finally suffocated me.

I can hardly live. I am so weak and feeble.
I can't see when this will end.
I'm so unhappy. I am exhausted.

Ah, God,
loosen my bonds, cool my brow,
take my hand, steady my step.
I have nothing left but you.
Do not disappoint me.

You are my buoy, my lighthouse, my home port.
Do not hide yourself.

You are my last hope, my last chance, my last helping hand.
Do not let me fall.

I need you so much!
I trust you... in spite of everything!
I love you!

Love is always ready to excuse, to trust, to hope and to endure whatever comes.

1 Corinthians 13, 7

Sickness of love

Lord,
things aren't going well between my partner and me.
We don't talk to each other any more,
in fact, we avoid each other.
I know there is someone else in his life.
That hurts me deeply.

What have I done to him
to make his love turn away from me?
What has happened to that faithfulness
we promised before you on our wedding day?
It has faded away, disappeared.

I no longer know what to say or do.
Only you can heal these wounds.
I trust in you.
Come, help us.

I love you with an everlasting love.
Isaiah 54, 8

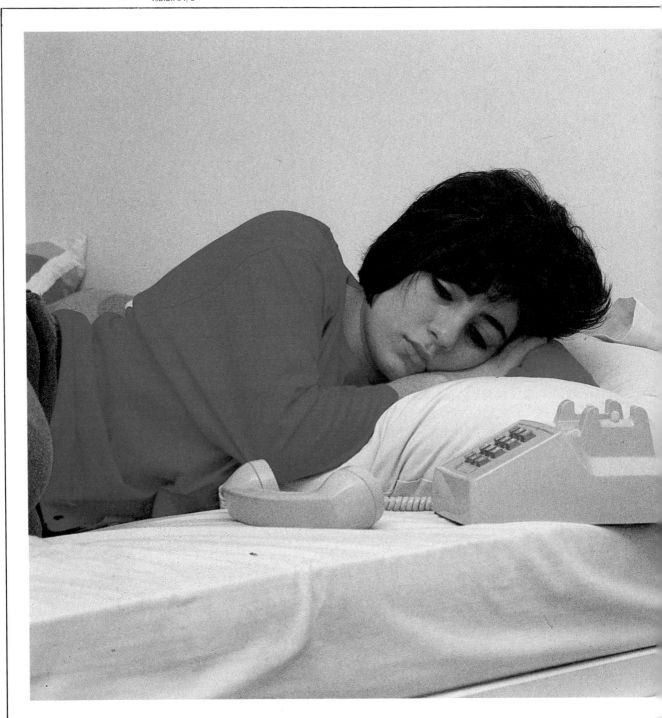

I am sick of living

Lord Jesus,
I'm getting along with problems.

Nothing goes right for me.
I am unemployed.
I'm living on social welfare.
I have no real friends.
Those I do have would drag me into evil
— alcohol, narcotics, stealing.
I'd like to do good
but I don't seem to have enough will-power.
I dislike myself.
I disgust myself.
I depress myself.
I'm fed up.

Help me.
Comfort me, encourage me.
I need it so much.

I trust you.

Amen.

There is more happiness in giving than receiving.

Acts 20, 35

The joy of giving

Lord,
while doing my usual chores,
I found time to phone Grandma today.
She is so lonely in her big house.
I packed two Christmas gifts for the poor.
I managed to walk to the hospital to visit a friend
who is worrying a good deal.

I'm proud of my day.
I wish all my days were as full of love as today.
Thank you for letting me help a little
and mostly for finding happiness in doing so.

Amen.

Mountains and hills, bless the Lord
Daniel 3, 75

The Lord of the woods

Lord,
it is pleasant outside, a lovely summer evening.
The breeze is quiet and the air fresh.

It just happened I went to the woods along the road.
I took a path lined with ferns and blue flowers.
The birds were already silent
and the squirrels had gone back to their nests.
I picked up and held a few pine needles,
I nibbled some winter-green leaves.
Then I leaned against a tall beech tree
showing its beautiful grey bark.

Ah God, how good I felt.
It seemed
the silence of the forest went deep into me
and you were at the very midst of it.
I wanted to stop time... I was so happy.
You were there in the calm and silence,
in the quiet and stillness
of the great trees and silent rocks.
I could almost touch you with my finger,
I felt you so close to me.

And life was so good... almost as in heaven!

You are my shepherd... you are at my side.
Psalm 23, 1, 4

I am always with you

Lord,
there are some tender mornings
when everything and everyone say, "I love you..."
There are sunlit noons
when nature as a whole tells you, "It is great to live..."
There are evenings of such beauty
that the very stars murmur,
"You will never stop being amazed..."

You feel you are walking on velvet carpets,
sailing on lakes like watered silk
or flying in deep blue skies.
You feel able to hold the world in your arms,
cut down forests, live a thousand lives.
It's wonderful.

But there also are nights of such darkness
that you ask unceasingly, "When will it end?"
There are winters of such sadness
that you groan like Job, "Perish the day I was born!"
There are nights of pain
when you shout yourself hoarse, "I can't bear any more!"

Your stomach is knotted up,
your head full of questions without answers,
your arms full of problems.
You are without hope, without energy, without inspiration.
You want to die.
You are fed up dragging through life. It's terrible!

In quiet days or stormy days,
stay with us.
We thank you for the light!
We beg help in the shadows!
May I never forget you when times are good
and never accuse you when times are bad.   Amen.

I thank you, Lord, with all my heart.
Psalm 9, 2

Prayer of a grandfather

Father,
you wanted me to live a long and good life.
I want to thank you for all the years.
You gave me children,
tall, strong, handsome.
I am proud of them.
In them, I see myself when I was their age.
And that gives me joy
and comforts my soul.

Then there are the grandchildren.
I take them on my knees and they hug me
and they don't find me old at all.
It's good to see yourself again
in your children and your grandchildren.

You who made us all, how pleased you must be
to see your likeness reproduced in us all.
I understand you a little
and... you understand me too, I know.
For everything and everyone,
I thank you with all my heart.

All you, works of the Lord, bless the Lord.
Daniel 3,57

Blessings

Through the clear stream that murmurs in the woods
and the heavy waterfall that flows down the hill,
I bless you, Lord.

Through the gentle rain that falls in April
and the violent storm that breaks in July,
I bless you, Lord.

Through the simple daisy which praises you throughout the day
and the white rose that will be faded by evening,
I bless you, Lord.

Through the lowly strawberry plant which is a treat in summer
and the good apple tree which gives of itself in the fall,
I bless you, Lord

Through the graceful swallow swooping in the sky
and the black-throated loon floating on the wave,
I bless you, Lord.

Through the youngster playing in the yard
and the old man rocking in the sunshine,
I bless you, Lord.

Through all the saints in heaven
and all the angels in paradise,
I bless you, Lord.

Pour out your hearts to God.

Psalm 62, 9

I wish...

Lord Jesus!

I wish
that our grandmothers were full of kindness and piety,
that our grandfathers might tell us of their experience and wisdom...

That small children would make the house cheerful
with their shouts, their races, their gentle love...
and that their parents would sit down
to play with them, talk to them and listen to them...

That older children could learn gently
about a beautiful, friendly world...
that teenagers would grow gradually
into independence and true freedom
and that young people would flourish cheerfully
in the sunshine of loving and giving...

That the poor might be helped,
the lonely visited
and the sick comforted...

That the daisy would grow in peace,
that wheat were not thrown into the sea
and that cars which are death traps would not explode...

I wish...

My soul is surfeited with troubles
Psalm 88, 4

Give me just a little breathing space

Almighty Father,
I never seem to stop trying to pull myself through.
With me, one misfortune doesn't wait for the next.
I never stop trying to get free.
I'm like a swimmer who gasps in water all the time.

When shall I be able to breathe easily?
When shall I be able to walk without stumbling?
I'd like so much to see a little sunlight between the clouds.

I can't go on.
I am always out of breath.
If only you would give me a breathing space,
just a little sunshine.

Don't leave me.
I count on you.
I need you.

You shall love your neighbor as yourself
Luke 10, 27

Sound self-love

Lord,
teach me how to love myself properly,
to accept myself as I am,
to weigh my qualities as well as my faults,
my performances as well as my failures.

It's hard for me to stop
to listen to the words which come from my own depths.
It's difficult to concentrate:
Hardships prevent me from
pondering over my inner life.
Yet I know
if I listened to my heart sing or weep,
if I listened to the voice which rises in me,
if I listened to you, who are closer to me than my very self,
I would be nourished in the depths of my being,
my life would take on consistency,
my way of living would be more united
and I would feel better.

Teach me, Lord, how to know myself,
to be attentive to my inner voice,
to know you in myself,
to love myself better.
Then surely I will be more at ease
to love you and to love others.

Amen.

You renew the face of the earth
Psalm 104, 30

For the earth

Yes, Lord,
let the rain come,
your heavy rain, warm and plentiful,
to make the earth fruitful
and let the seed sprout.

Yes, Lord,
let the sunlight come,
your beautiful sunlight, glowing and golden,
to make the soil smile
and bring forth fruit.

Yes, Lord,
let the wind come,
your powerful wind, mighty and vigorous,
to dry the earth
and give it plentiful life!

Trust in the Lord with all your heart.
Proverbs 3, 5

Stress

Oh Father,
it seems I look crushed with stress.
I worry for nothing.
I am not only occupied but preoccupied.
I am destroying myself
little by little.

You who live in the garden of my soul,
be my strong tranquillity;
keep me peaceful and serene.
Give me enough faith and hope
to trust you in everything.

I surrender myself to you.
Take me in your arms.
Free me from distress.
Into your hands I commend my spirit,
my heart, my body,
my whole being.

Amen.

Great has been your kindness to me, Lord.
Psalm 86, 13

I just come to say goodnight

Lord Jesus,
I've come to greet you,
to say goodnight.
I hope it was a good day for you too.
Sometimes I feel you must be tired
listening to everyone,
all of us telling you our concerns,
especially because most of the time
we bring you our problems.

My problems,
you know them better than I do.
I won't tell you about them.
While saying goodnight to you,
I just want to mention
I love you the most I can
and, above all, I welcome once more the love
you never cease to give me.

It's wonderful to be in love, you know.
And, after that,
I need only be here,
saying nothing at all.
Goodnight!

Table of prayers

Printed and bound in Canada

IMPRIMERIE
L'ÉCLAIREUR
BEAUCEVILLE
12420